AF366449

One easy guide on reducing anxiety and coping with examination stress

ExLibric

MARÍA TERESA VICTORIA

One easy guide on reducing anxiety
and coping with examination stress

EXLIBRIC

ANTEQUERA 2021

MARÍA TERESA VICTORIA

BE

mindful

One easy guide on reducing anxiety and coping with examination stress

Índice

Prologue

María Teresa Roura Vivas has been trying to help her students get their best results in standardised tests since the Junta de Andalucia new regulations in 2012. It was a major task for her to try and **de-stress classroom climates** during examination periods for which reason she trained her students well beforehand on how to **regulate** high emotions and feelings of anxiety.

As a professional it felt extremely frustrating for her to see well-prepared students, who had worked hard all through their academic course, failing to sit their final exams or simply just giving in at the last minute or not turning up (specially at their oral examinations). This gave her the determination to continue her research on discovering optimal ways, tools and strategies that students could hold on to during **high peaks of anxiety** in exam period. **Coping mechanisms** to deal with those hard instances of examination stress and finally manage to **concentrate and focus** on doing their best and getting the best result possible. That is how *Be Mindful* was born.

Based on the PINEP program (below) which she became familiar with during her postgraduate Master's studies at the University of Málaga (2018), *One easy guide on reducing anxiety and coping with examination stress* offers applicants to standardised ESL tests worldwide, a brief introduction to the origins of the millenary practice of Mindfulness where the user will learn how to befriend silence and slowly encounter their own ability to focus using simple concentration techniques that will help them become more aligned and focused through basic breathing exercises.

Potential examinees will also navigate through uncomplicated attention and emotion self-regulation practices that will help them later on during high moments of examination stress or anxiety when they need the support. The intention of all this being to achieve the best result possible. These comments from students acquiring the practice speak by themselves: 'I feel relaxed and energized after the practice, fully recharged to start work' or 'Great practice. It gets easier and feels better each time. These techniques are not only good for oral exams!' and 'Mindfulness practices help clear my mind and fully concentrate' as well as 'Mindfulness practice helps us to be more calm and confident. A very positive experience indeed'.

As the author herself points out one good benefit of Mindfulness practice that comes alongside decreased stress is **productivity**, which will surely stay with those who decide to put this useful guide in their pockets. The reader of these guidelines for language users and university applicants of standardised English tests may grow **more creative**, will be shown some cultivating **resilience** practices and learn about **self-compassion** becoming a must-have, or how **loving kindness** exercises might help their own personal and professional growth and self-development.

"With the idea of facilitating the regulation of emotions through mindfulness, the Mindfulness and Emotional Intelligence Program was developed. PINEP can be defined as a conscious emotional management program whose objective is to help participants in the process of `learning to feel´, and to provide individuals with sufficient resources to accompany their own emotional states and those of third parties. This could result in their becoming aware of the mechanisms which inhibit the achievement of personal goals in situations of high emotional intensity, and thus restore the adaptive value of an emotion. This implies that PINEP, through the formal and informal practice of mindfulness, helps the individual to deal with highly emotional situations" by *Ramos NS; Enríquez, H and Recondo, O. (2012) Inteligencia Emocional Plena. Mindfulness y la gestión emocional de las emociones. (Edición Revisada). Barcelona: Kairós.*

Ph. D. Natalia Sylvia Ramos-Díaz, Director of Master Studies in the Mindfulness and Emotional Intelligence Program, Professor at the Faculty of Psychology, University of Málaga (Spain).

Foreword

The Emotional Intelligence courses undertaken since the beginning of my career as an English teacher came to a turning-point during the PINEP Program run at the Teachers Training Centre CEP Marbella-Coin in 2018 (Reference: 182923GES251).

The contributions of the PINEP program proved to be the most interesting to top up the experience I had built up as an emotional intelligence practitioner in the English classroom since 1993. The program's proposals and techniques were developed within B1 Certificate candidates in 2018 focusing mainly and most importantly on how to improve my students speaking competence and skills. So some innovative Mindfulness and Emotional Intelligence activities and interventions were brought into the classroom to build up new strategies for the students to tackle their final speaking examination tasks.

The 2018 experience helped candidates [1] FOCUS ONLY on the interactive task with their partner, and nothing else (nervousness, the unexpected, unwanted topics, unusual partners, etc); [2] GET RID of distractions and/or insecurities; [3] BECOME AWARE of their own speaking productions and of pointing out at the most useful items to deliver their best Monologues and Dialogues; [4] REDUCE stress and, [5] CONCENTRATE on speech. The candidates feedback after their practices was interesting: (a) they felt more capable of managing their emotions under pressure, (b) their self esteem was risen, (c) they were more confident when delivering Monologues, (e) they overcame block-outs, (f) their actual performance improved resulting in a genuine interactive task where a dialogue is not two monologues, (g) they were able to focus on breathing until their "mind manages to come back" to the written instructions they need to read and follow, (h) they were able to create conscious Monologues "with a beginning a middle and an end" even closed up sometimes by really witty phrases and quotes, and (i) last but not least, they seemed to **enjoy the creative process** of building up an intelligent interactive task here and now, which managed to engage their audience in a good improvised little theatre play.

Students admitted to having become **more aware** of their mistakes and how to improve for the future, learning how to build up their own strategies for when they undoubtedly will block out, growing more aware of present time (3-5min tasks), learning how to "open–develop–close up" their speech without distractions, and most importantly, learning how to register bodily techniques through Mindfulness practices to help them manage their emotions under stress.

From the examiner's viewpoint I can say that the PINEP program developed my own ability to focus on the positives. The positives become more visible, thus resulting in an interesting more balanced perception of the candidates speaking performances with better final results. And this was just the beginning. What came next was the content of this guide, that is, research work on Mindfulness in Education that closed up my Mater's Studies and some practical instructions and interventions in the classroom following a brief introduction to Mindfulness concepts and definition. May the reader please notice the references to audios and/or videos can be found in the same sessions of the Be Mindful proposal in my website www.mindfulenglish.net

Mindfulness: definition and concept

Before this easy guide on reducing anxiety and coping with examination stress is presented for applicants to standardised English tests to learn how to manage their emotions and find **mechanisms to cope with anxiety and examination stress,** we would like to name two references for a definition of Mindfulness.

Being an English literature lover myself, the first reference to Mindfulness here is this wisely brought up metaphor that Jon Kabat-Zinn himself uses to describe what Mindfulness may look like: it is "Much Ado About Nothing" (explained below). The second reference could not be other than the basis of our "Mindfulness and Emotional Intelligence program" Master's research at the University of Málaga (Ramos, 2019) developed with the idea of facilitating the regulation of emotions through Mindfulness as it was explained in the prologue.

The founder of Mindfulness paraphrases Shakespeare at the "Mindfulness to face pain, stress and illness" conference (Faculty of Medicine of the Complutense University of Madrid, 2016) to describe how much benefit can be obtained from "doing nothing". When we stop to attend to the breath and observe the mind, thoughts, emotions and sensations "apparently doing nothing" many things happen that we are not normally aware of. We realise that our mind does not stop, that what the mind is really doing is thinking, remembering, planning all the time, and we become aware of the neural network of our brain and everything that is linked to it. A whole world of self-knowledge, self-regulation, and responsibility for ourselves raises up from that "doing nothing" or rather "non-doing".

Jon Kabat-Zinn names relevant aspects of Mindfulness as "Befriending silence" that describes how through silence we enter the domain of "Being", which takes us to the territory of "Well-being" in our own company. And how through silence we can connect with our own self-care, being able to take responsibility for and become more participative of our own healings instead of delegating to Medicine. He talks about initiating a "Love affair with life itself" as we grow more aware of our well- being and happiness in enjoying this present moment that is all we have.

An introduction to programs and interventions in Mindfulness

Apart from the field of health in general and medical diseases and psychological disorders in particular, it is worth highlighting various fields of application of programs and interventions in Mindfulness, such as business or entrepreneurship, sports, prisons, military, judicial, security and education. The latter will be widely deployed further.

Mindfulness is currently slowly being implemented in business environments where leaders are seemingly becoming more aware of how safety is actually linked to health, and taking care of their workers' mental health is a growing need. Introductory trainings to the practice of Mindfulness are starting to be offered widely in workplaces.

Mindfulness techniques have been used for years in a wide variety of philosophical and religious systems. During the last decades it has undergone a distillation process that has resulted in practices widely used in various spheres of life in a secular way. The techniques were introduced in Medicine in 1979 by John Kabat-Zinn, emeritus professor at the University of Massachusetts, and since then it has been having application also in different fields such as Psychology, Business or the Military – more recently in the Educational field as it will be revealed in the last chapter.

Mindfulness and the natural rhythms of Life

Mindfulness can be considered a practice, a state or a trait. We can have a meditative intention and (1) do Mindfulness practices through different known techniques, or we can also (2) have "mindful moments" in which we bring more awareness to the present time, and (3) it can finally become a trait of personality where we adopt a more conscious attitude in general in our life.

The main characteristic of Mindfulness is to pay attention and bring awareness to the vital experience of the present, where what matters is not so much the object of attention but the quality of that attention. This attention has special features such as observing with an intention, with an openness to receive whatever is happening in the present moment (without trying to control it at all, just watching and letting go).

When we stop and observe perhaps we can discover that we are doing one task while mentally we are in another, and we may even be surprised that at the end of the day we have hardly been "present" in what we have done. We move in " autopilot" guided by beliefs and habits that we unconsciously reproduce over and over again, with the inconvenience of disconnecting ourselves from reality by living in "automation" when going from task to task, maybe making mistakes or having accidents by being completely absent. There is also the inconvenience of stress caused by not living the natural rhythms of Life.

Suffering can weigh us down

Mindfulness is also "understanding" that suffering is part of life. The way in which we relate to that suffering and our way of approaching it, can cause us stress or dissatisfaction. This suffering is in our mind and it does not weigh anything but it can weigh us down a lot like Jon Kabat-Zinn explains. Being aware as well of our own happiness will help us find a place of well-being with ourselves and with others.

Through the practice of Mindfulness or paying attention to the present moment, two important features appear: the awareness of that present moment and equanimity. Equanimity can help us be more balanced the more we do the practice itself. For that we can follow some guidelines with different objects of attention, for example, (1) attention to exteroceptive sensations or the senses, (2) attention to interoceptive and proprioceptive sensations or the body, and (3) attention to thoughts, which are the three constituent elements of emotions.

Some benefits can be obtained from the practice of Mindfulness as proven by scientific research showing the effects on the prefrontal cortex of the brain responsible for the executive functions.

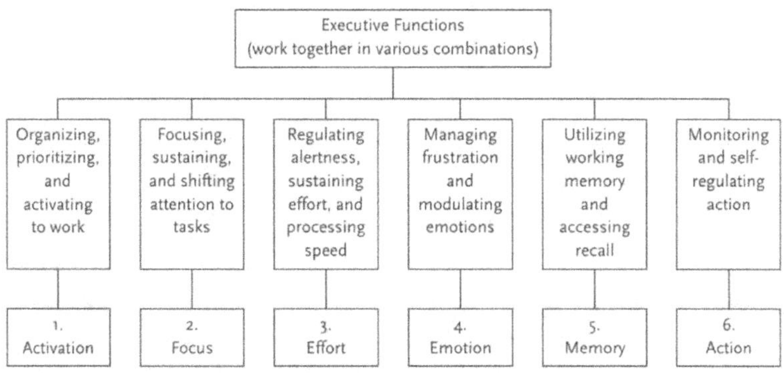

Figure 1. "Executive functions" from *The Unfocused Mind* by Thomas Brown

Some of the aspects related to well-being that are developed by the stimulation of the prefrontal cortex through the practice of Mindfulness include (1) body regulation that coordinates the appropriate alertness and energy levels for each situation, (2) acquisition of self-awareness that contributes to creating our own life history by connecting attention to the present moment with memories of the past and images of the future that are actually key elements to build positive social relationships, (3) emotional regulation that manages to activate our life experiences in an appropriate way avoiding to put ourselves in chaotic situations (or situations that may overwhelm us) and even states of depression or feeling that our life has no meaning, (4) and modulation of fear developing the ability to calm down and relax, and even "unlearn" the paths that lead us to dreaded feared catastrophic scenarios.

An introduction to begin your practice

Some authors define the practice of Mindfulness as "the sustained and non-evaluative attention to the experience as it is at the present moment, without judging or assessing it and without reacting to it" (Ramos, Recondo and Enríquez, 2012, p.21).

The fact that the practice is "Intentional" becomes essential to grow more aware, so it is ideal to create an adequate space where we can be calm without being disturbed, or even accustom the rest of the family members or people who live at home to respect that mindful moment that is becoming part of our daily habits. Mindfulness has currently been "sold" as a package that comes with rituals, postures, objects and images, which as a matter of fact, are completely unnecessary for the practice itself. The intention is simple: to observe and become aware of ourselves in an attempt to self-regulate and find a better place in our own lives in the most responsible manner possible.

A posture that keeps us in balance between alertness and relaxation is enough, either sitting in a chair or lying on the floor, or adopting the Buddha position. The important thing is to make sure that we are well anchored in the here and now by connecting our body with the earth (feet on the floor) and with the sky (head upright) through the central axis of a comfortably supported spine that self-elevates itself.

By focusing on the breath we will be able to notice what comes up from the experience. Trying to control or force whatever comes up to disappear and return to the breath is not recommended but on the contrary we are letting whatever comes and goes just "Be" in the background with the breath as a referential focus.

To stabilize the breath we can help ourselves with anchors or labels that indicate the experience as a "sound" if we hear something, or "itching" if we have the bodily sensation, or "sadness" if this emotion appears, for instance. The labels "good" or "bad" would rather pass judgment so we will avoid those.

Paying attention to our body can give us a lot of information about ourselves, and being aware of this can contribute to our own physical and emotional care, also to better decision-making and choice of paths in our lives (after all, the body has been called our second brain). We can also foster empathy for others by recognizing in our peers intense emotions such as anguish or euphoria that we have experienced ourselves. During body scan practices we may also become aware of some discomfort that has gone unnoticed before, and even more important, perhaps realise where our own boundaries lie (yoga, for instance, can be an interesting practice to literally and metaphorically recognize how far we can go).

Portability

Mindfulness practice doesn't have to be static. It is a tool that can be taken wherever we go regardless of what we are doing or where we are. We can bring observation and awareness while we are opening a door, for example, or when picking up the phone. We can easily have a moment of awareness of our breath, our body and our mind in everyday life since "becoming aware" does not really require a great effort and can enrich the experience in the simplicity of day to day life by getting us to interact with the world in a different way.

When becoming aware of the present moment we can choose to act differently and this will undoubtedly have a positive impact on our lives since we are training ourselves to live our emotions with greater clarity and equanimity. The small successes promote the feeling of security and confidence which can gradually make that fear dissipate of being overwhelmed by life's events. Mindfulness can put us in a safer inner place.

Through the practice of Mindfulness we can have more experiences of caring and kindness, of love and compassion, and fewer experiences of anger, worry, or feelings that something is missing in our lives. We can grow more precise in recognizing the emotions that come and go as guests in our home and accept them as they come and go. Even when these are difficult emotions that will open doors to other places and contribute to better self-knowledge.

Alertness

Our brain is programmed to put us in a situation of alert to what may be happening in the vicinity to react to the slightest threat. Within our brain inhabits the amygdala, which is the vigilant guardian that wants to protect us from negative experiences. Unfortunately, brain connections do not have the scanning and recording of positive experiences as a priority and these tend to fall into oblivion as a general rule. The practice of Mindfulness can help us bring awareness also of the memorable positive experiences (or even those at least that are only neutral) which can compensate and balance our existence in a more holistic way.

The last will be first

Interestingly, for this practitioner the central core of the Mindfulness experience is the so-called emotion regulation or emotional self-regulation. So becoming aware of how an emotion leads to a thought or a thought generates an emotion, in a cyclical way, can help us get out of a situation in which we have unconsciously stagnated and that is affecting us considerably.

Our cognitive processes were the last ones to develop in our brain, which is to say that self-control or self-regulation is the most recent resource of the capabilities of a human being and therefore the first to suffer some kind of disability when resources are deficient.

Furthermore, cultivating self-compassion is a new resource that will help us at times when this ability for self-regulation fails. So being kind to ourselves can be convenient as keeping in mind that we have been repeating very old trained habits since childhood would also be convenient. "Unlearning" those habits does take time and practice. Some intense emotions such as anger, for instance, are not easy to navigate and we generally fall into personality patterns when we encounter them, such us overreacting, attacking or withdrawing from the experience, or even suppressing the emotion directly. That moment when we realize what happened then comes too late and we end up regretting the total experience as a whole. The good news is that we can strengthen our muscles by exercising. Self-regulation skills can also be trained through the practice of Mindfulness.

Stimulus - Mindfulness - Response vs Stimulus - Reaction

Mindfulness provides a distance from the stimulus that allows us to respond instead of (over) reacting. So by allowing ourselves to observe our emotion without judgment we can find in Mindfulness a powerful tool especially in the face of intense emotions that can make others feel uncomfortable which are generally labeled as "bad", "not correct" or "inappropriate".

When a difficult emotion manifests itself with great force it can motivate us to do something in the face of an injustice. With the practice of Mindfulness, though, we can learn to wisely align this emotion, be able to let the experience flourish inside of us, and determine what form we want it to take as our outward-facing expression.

We will be training ourselves in the ability of acting in a way that seems most appropriate to us when an emotional experience occurs, rather than letting the experience itself take control of ourselves. More specifically with negative experiences, as mentioned above, we may get stuck forgetting all those positive experiences that also surround us (but that we take for granted) so the negative feeling can then become chronic to the point that it can reach a psychological decline related to the stresses of life that may be accompanied by painful diseases.

We must remind ourselves then that positive emotions can be cultivated as well through the Mindfulness experience. Thus leading us to express some gratitude for, and opening up the spectrum to all the beautiful things that happen in our lives, which may bring balance to what causes us damage or produces discomfort. It has been shown that cultivating these positive emotions can become our lifeline in times of extreme distress and mental restlessness. In fact, positive emotions stimulate the parasympathetic nervous system that complements the sympathetic nervous system installed in the brain that makes us alert and warns us of threats.

As well as our body, our brain would contract when facing an emotion like fear, or rage, or anger and it is much more difficult to stay fully present in the experience of what is happening. Suddenly the entire universe seems to be against us and our view of the world becomes so narrow that at times the feeling becomes claustrophobic.

The feeling of openness and the ability to learn how to take care of ourselves and others can also be felt in the body and in the mind as a counterpoint, taking the form of light, relaxation, space and grounding, which is what the practice of Mindfulness can bring to our lives.

The riddle wrapped in a mystery inside an enigma

Before this theoretical framework of Mindfulness comes to an end we would like to underpin two main concepts that have been found fundamental by the author.

During our first sessions at the University of Málaga postgraduate Master's degree in Emotion regulation through Mindfulness practices, one question always raised in my perplexed mind after the theories that had been excellently presented by outstanding lecturers from different fields and backgrounds that visited us: how to adopt that mindful attitude and manage to bring equanimity in this frantic world.

The answer delivered by the professors and doctors was always the same again: practice. The instructions of all the speakers were always directed towards that place where you can sit well and feel at ease, and you can dedicate yourself to practising a few minutes every day. That is how my Mindfulness corner was born, impregnated now with this special energy that is felt by all as one enters, and where it seems my long-awaited key to equanimity has been found.

Where this phrase wisely introduced to me by one of the speakers "I am not my emotion" is repeated over and over again, helping me to focus on "being" by distancing myself from the emotion. To learn how to act a jad more evenly out there in this frantic world, hoping that one day the equanimous attitude with capital letters will be reached for ever is the intention. The key, we find is equanimity, the speaker said over and over again, adding that still, after so much energy and intention he puts into his practice, sometimes he also loses it and then regrets.

But at least I have now learned not to scourge myself for what may have happened and treat myself with patience and Love instead, and keep an eye wide open on the road not make the same mistake again. And should it happen once again, keep trying and keep learning, and treat one another lovingly at each fall as self- compassion is an essential component for growth, and the emotion in which all other emotions are embraced, the greatest, is Love.

Be Mindful is originally a tailor-made guide to help Official Language School students in Spain reduce anxiety and cope with examination stress. The guidelines can perfectly be also followed by other students or examination candidates of standardised English tests all over the world. After the eight sessions that follow, our students will have learned some long term strategies that may help them achieve their best performance in final examinations.

SESSION ONE: FROM DOING TO BEING

SESSION TWO: BEFRIENDING SILENCE

SESSION THREE: ATTENTION REGULATION

SESSION FOUR: EMOTION REGULATION

SESSION FIVE: TIME MANAGEMEN

SESSION SIX: CULTIVATING RESILIENCE

SESSION SEVEN: LOVING KINDNESS

SESSION EIGHT: CLOSING UP

Introduction

Mindfulness is already being practiced in most acknowledged Universities in the USA , the United Kingdom or Australia where it has been proven that students can acquire coping mechanisms to deal with stress during exam period, among others.

The students who have attended the sessions claim that their *self-awareness* improves, their ability to pay *attention* is better, their *concentration skills* are enhanced, their *cognitive flexibility* is improved, they develop their own *learning strategies,* they learn how to plan *their work and study,* they get *better results,* they manage to *reduce anxiety,* and they become more *resilient.*

It is interesting to find out that Three-minute-breathing-space practices taught in the university classroom report fewer episodes of mind wandering and distractibility, and more than half the students used the practice also outside the course.

Some programs and interventions currently followed at Universities are:

CAMBRIDGE UNIVERSITY provides a wide range of daily practice of Mindfulness as well as 8-week MBSR programs and three-month workshops with a focus on concentration skills, how to handle exam anxiety, decision making, resting and de-stressing plus time management during exam period.

OXFORD UNIVERSITY Mindfulness Based Stress Reduction [MBSR] programs started in 2011 with outstanding results and hundreds of students participating.

HARVARD UNIVERSITY offers Mindfulness sessions on a daily basis, a 4-week Mindfulness program, and the official MBSR eight-week program twice a year.

STANFORD UNIVERSITY organises specially designed 6-week programs for their first year students twice a year; second and third year students can attend Mindfulness workshops which will provide credits to their curricula. Mindfulness sessions are also available.

A three-minute breathing practice can be easy and really useful when you need to be calm (i.e. exam period). All we need to do is sit comfortably, with your head up right, feet touching the floor, hands resting on your lap and breath in slowly, feeling the air through our nose, then breathe out. Rest in your breath coming in and out. Perhaps hear the sounds around and inside us, and focusing on the present moment, come back to your breathing, nicely and gently, as many times as the mind goes into the thoughts stream.

Session one: from doing to being

As the founder of Mindfulness explains, one of the hardest things for us human beings is «not to do». And when we stop we will realise that as soon as we get quiet the mind starts to do what the mind does all the time, which is t-h-i-n-k-i-n-g.

The mind is just like a Thinking Machine. It never stops. So when we practice Mindfulness we are cultivating access to awareness, pure awareness, as opposed to getting lost in the thoughts stream. It is not a special estate that we have to get to, it is a core capacity that we have, which is part of being human but that we ignore all the time.

Mindfulness is not shutting off our thinking, there is not some special place where we don't think. So if we try to put ourselves in some special place where we don't think we're going to give ourselves a gigantic headache, because thinking is one of the things that the mind does.

That doesn't mean we can't be in a relationship with our thinking. Mindfulness is about "relationality", when we practice Mindfulness we learn to be in a relationship with inner experience and outer experience.

Mindfulness is not about breathing and it's not about any other object that we can pay attention to. Mindfulness is about attending itself. More and more, research is showing that as you develop functional connectivity through Mindfulness what is being functionally connected is the posterior singular cortex in the limbic system with the prefrontal cortex, the cortical areas that involve emotional regulation and attention regulation, perspective taking and executive functions.

With the practice of Mindfulness we can actually transform towards greater presence, greater wakefulness, greater potential for actually acting in ways that are more in alignment with our own purpose and the actual circumstances that we find ourselves in.

So the invitation this first session is to try these instructions adapted from Jon Kabat-Zinn's for our first Mindfulness practices.

1. Let's establish ourselves in a posture that for you embodies wakefulness and dignity. Don't lean back against the back of the chair but sit up so that you are more autonomous and the spine self elevates out of your seat.

2. And let's bring our awareness to the fact that we are breathing.

3. Let's bring awareness to the feeling, to the sensations of the breath moving in and out of the body. And ride like a surfer on the waves of your own in- breath and out-breath with full awareness with full attention.

4. So the invitation is to rest in the experience of the breath moving in and out of the body as a whole. Sitting here. Breathing. There is no place to go. Nothing to do. And no special place to attain. And at the same time the experience you are having is fantastically special. Because it is Life expressing itself. In this only moment we ever have.

5. You feel fine and at a certain time you've forgotten about the breath and it's long out of your mind and you've fallen into the thought stream being carried away to some place and then you discover it… So being aware of what's in your mind in this moment when you discover that it's not on the breath means you're back! And then gently and lovingly and kindly - without judging yourself for

it in any way – let's call your attention back into the body or the belly or wherever you've been feeling the breath sensations most vividly. And if the mind wanders a hundred thousand times each time you notice what's on your mind and come back without judging, without condemning yourself, without pursuing the thoughts. Just continually reconnecting with awareness itself in the body.

6. What we are doing here, and another way to say it, is "befriending silence", we are befriending Stillness.

7. So how is your attention in this very moment of now. How is it in the body right in this moment seeing that you can know that directly through "awareness"… not through thinking. More like through sensing and feeling. How is it in what we call "the mind" right in this moment… Is there impatience, boredom, a lot of thinking, little thinking?. Is there emotional reactivity?

8. And whatever is here, just knowing that, not conceptually, not cognitively but with awareness itself, underneath words inside of this silent wakefulness, this silent knowing, is here.

9. Rest in what we might call the open spaciousness of awareness itself and let whatever arises in the space of awareness be met and known. Just like a mirror in some sense reflects whatever comes before, but it's not attached to following whatever comes or to clinging on to whatever comes. So rest in this awareness, taking up residency.

10. As if you said to yourself "Ok, now I'm just going to live here for now. Since "now" is the only moment you ever get to live! And that awareness can include the body, feelings, thoughts, sounds. But it is not caught by any of

it because it is simply pure wakefulness. And knowing is also in some sense "not knowing" or "knowing of how much we actually don't know". And being equally at home with not knowing. Stay there, and finally gently and lovingly and kindly let's call your attention to this place, and let's listen to the sounds and let's open our eyes very slowly so we get back to the room.

Session two: befriending silence

In the previous session we learned that Mindfulness is not a special estate that you have to get to. What we are doing is rather, cultivating access to awareness, becoming more aware of when we get lost in the thought stream and by practicing, learning how to redirect and focus.

I absolutely adore the expression «Befriending silence» which is, as a matter of fact, growing more comfortable with being with your own company. Befriending silence when you are sitting there, just breathing, can be practiced by focusing on your thoughts and surrounding sounds ["Mindfulness Meditation Listening by Mark Williams and Danny Penman" audio available].

You may wonder what we are doing this for, at first, and I can tell you that my experience is (by practising this exercise of listening to the sounds) my ability to focus became bigger and better, and the most amazing was to start noticing that more and more people were asking how I could hear that (my sense of hearing was growing more acute) or «how come you have seen me coming» like colleagues would exclaim «if I have walked in so silently!». I noticed I was cultivating awareness of things happening around: conversations, movements, expressions, emotions and behaviours.

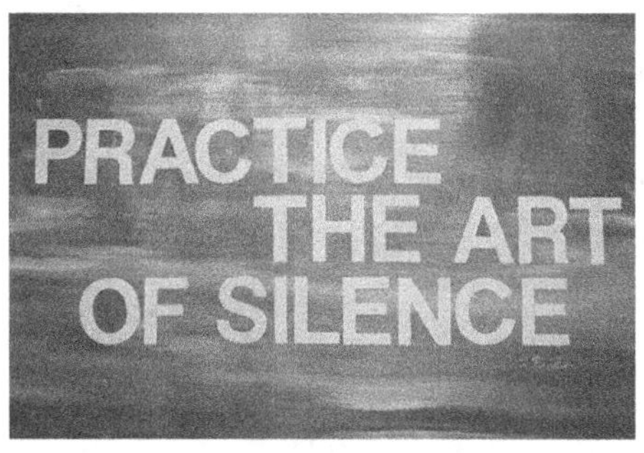

By befriending silence through sitting, breathing, and paying attention to our thoughts, to the sounds, or focusing on sensations when scanning our body, we are developing this ability to connect to our inner and outer experiences. There is no need to sit for long to begin with, however, you may notice that every day you stay a little longer and what is happening is that you are becoming more comfortable with being in silence, more comfortable in your own company, more comfortable with yourself and more aware of the others.

You might be wondering what *Befriending silence* really has to do with exams!! And the interesting thing is that the exercises can actually help us outside the practice as well. Our brain is getting trained to redirect and focus and the exercise works for building up our concentration skills when we are preparing for our exams or right there when we are about to make a final decisive speech in front of the examiners and emotions have taken over. The practice helps us reduce anxiety as our body and mind will have memorised how to restore calmness breathing slowly and surely thanks to the usual practice. Repeat these practices regularly and see if anything changes.

Session three: attention regulation

If you can remember the first few minutes of the 1994 highest-grossing British film Four Weddings and a Funeral when we all laughed with Charles and his sister (Hugh Grant and Charlotte Coleman) jumping out of bed at the beep of the alarm clock as they were running late for the wedding [video clip available] you will be able to imagine what living on auto-pilot would be like as opposed to bringing awareness to our actions, which is what we do when we practice Mindfulness.

How many times have you found yourself jumping out of bed, having breakfast, getting in the car, going to work, finishing work, picking up the kids, going home, cooking food, having dinner, going to bed without even realising where all the time has gone. And the same thing the day after. And the day after. And one year later. Then ten years later.

It happens all the time, in every day life, a bit like in the classic movie Groundhog Day we wake up every morning and follow an automatic daily routine. Sometimes we are not even aware of when we missed our exit on the motorway or what this tv program we have been watching for the last half hour is about. We don't know sometimes why we are doing the things we do, or why we are spending time with these people around, or why we are on this trip when we would have rather stayed at home, or the opposite. We are not actually fully aware of what we do. We just keep doing things automatically without really questioning much. And then ... one day, maybe, we find ourselves in a position we didn't choose that is making ourselves very unhappy or is adding stress to our existence or is bringing us down badly. And we then wonder how we got there. This is called unawareness.

When and how did I choose this?

To stop living on autopilot we simply need just that: to stop. Stop and see. Stop and feel. Stop and make that conscious decision. Stop and ask ourselves do I really want this, do I really need to, will this really bring happiness into my life, am I aware of the consequences. The intention of Mindfulness practice is to bring consciousness to our movements, to the moments we are living, the decisions we are making, the people we are sharing our precious time with. *We befriend silence* just to pay full attention and be at enormous ease. To become more aware and walk the right path for us preventing ourselves from suddenly finding that we are all trapped within the wrong situation, place or people when we had no intention whatsoever to actually get there! I like to call this tool my personal GPS system.

Contrary to what is often assumed we don't necessarily need to formally sit still on a cushion to practice. There is a variety of Attention Regulation practices as the following:

INFORMAL PRACTICE

We can increase focus by incorporating present-time awareness into movement, for instance, walking mindfully to work. We can bring awareness to the sounds and smells around, to how we feel or what we say, we can investigate and become more aware of how our body works and feels. We can choose one activity that we will be performing during the day as a mindful bell, for example, answering a phone call, cooking or having a shower, and take a conscious shift to direct our mind towards appreciating the present moment with full attention noticing our breathing, emotions, and body as it is performing the task.

We can also increase our awareness throughout the day with portable Mindfulness practices like simply stopping what you are doing for a little while and taking a few minutes to just pay full attention to an object and become more aware of the present moment. Try to discipline your mind while your mind may try to go to the past or the future. Become more aware of what is going on around you but also inside of you. So you can better understand your own habits and emotional states.

We may as well pick a time to practice Mindful eating (during one meal a day or when having our favourite drink) and bring in all our senses to what we notice – sight, smell, touch, taste, and sounds, any thoughts, feelings or emotions that arise... and keep a journal about this experience if we really get into it. Appreciating and noticing our body sensations will give us information, for example, of when to have food and drink and how much we actually need.

FORMAL PRACTICE

One other misconception about Mindfulness practices is that we just sit back and relax to disconnect when it is rather the opposite, the suggestion is sitting up and if possible, not to lean against the back of the chair and to connect to our inner and outer experiences. Other formal instances include standing and lying down practices.

The intention we want to put into the practice will guide us, for example, if we choose to do our formal practice as the day begins in the morning we may put a particular intention into the day to replace «the autopilot» and focus on what we are here for, what we want our day to begin like, from where will I act today, what would I (not) like to bring into my life today. Mindfulness gives us the freedom of not-having-to-be but to feel and choose the best solution that suits what is happening to me here and now by connecting to this present moment.

> *Between stimulus and response there is a space. In that space is our power to choose our response. In our response lies our growth and our freedom» (Viktor E. Frankl)*

Session four: emotion regulation

We have probably just arrived at the most intriguing destination on Mindfulness journeys, at least, it certainly was the case for me. Once our mindful routines and habits are settled, the big question is

how can I not let myself get carried away by «mindlessness» emotions that will have unwanted side effects

To me this was the «riddle-wrapped-in-a-mystery-inside-an-enigma». "A videoclip is available where psychologist Paul Ekman explains well the process of emotions, how to grow more aware of them and how to ACT instead of REAct (or OVERreact as it usually is the case) when we are overtaken by anger, rage, love or fear, for instance, and are pretty much oblivious of the consequences.

To expand the gap between STIMULUS and RESPONSE we need to bring awareness through Observation and Practice, which we can do with the help of Mindfulness exercises. The more aware we become of our thoughts, feelings and emotions, the more capable we will be of consciously deciding what to do.

This Emotion and Feeling wheel will help us recognise a feeling or an emotion we cannot quite name and we can come back to it every time we need, even more so, when we become aware of our reply «good» or «bad» to the question «how does that make you feel?». Good and Bad can certainly be explained in more detail and will give us (and others) more specific information about an issue that will help clarify, unwind

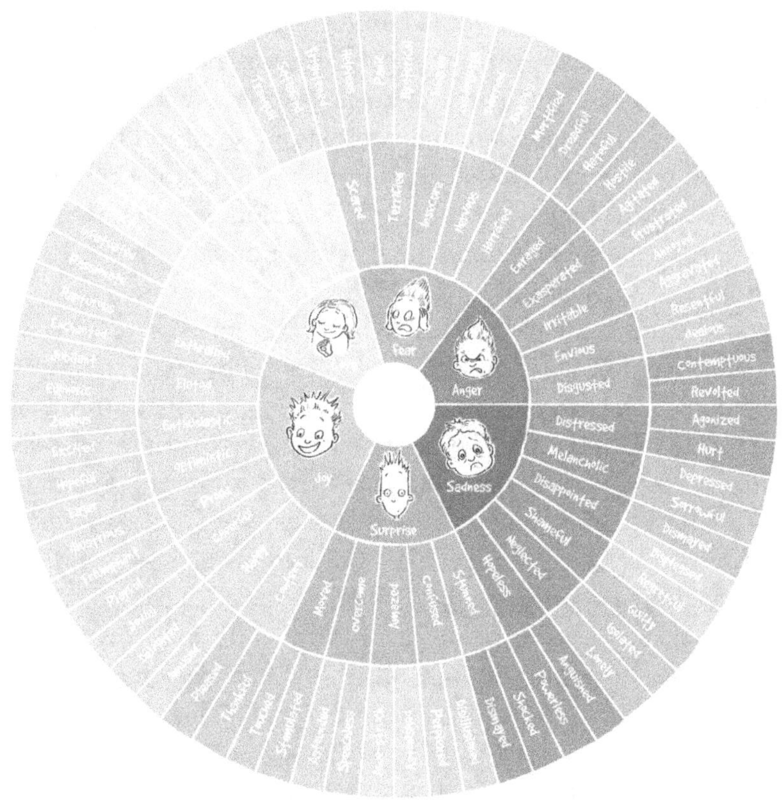

and break habit loops. By identifying the emotion we can try and stop the stream that usually follows by choosing a different path, sometimes retrieving from «the fire» others bringing in alternatives or simply remaining quiet doing nothing.

Consciously choosing a "response" instead of "reacting" is not an easy task, I have to say. I have (over) reacted many times even after years of awareness practices. It is a long term trip with valuable benefits that comes with good doses of compassion as we will study in the Loving kindness session. And I would like to say now that it is worth the effort and will help you arrive in that place where you actually want to be. Slowly and surely. So all of the above applied in the context of a stressful situation as it could be «To make a speech in front of a board of examiners» makes sense when we can feel the emotion arriving as waves coming to the shore, and before that emotion takes over, we can SEE it – BREATHE it – MANAGE it.

Because we have gradually become more aware of how feelings and emotions reflect in our body (see attention regulation) we may realise in a split second that stress has suddenly become our guest when we were just peacefully sitting there before the examiners right about to begin to talk. The big difference now is that we have become more aware of ourselves after regular mindfulness practices and we can acknowledge the feeling, embrace it and accept that this guest will be here with me for a little while until my whole organ system resets through breathing (maybe I need to go let my eyes out of focus for a little while, drink some water, apply some colour to this bit or let the breeze in through that window). The fact is that just by opening up a space and welcoming this «unexpected» guest by acknowledging it and embracing it, we are already on the move as opposed to getting paralyzed by restlessness. We have practised the «focusing on the air we breathe in – and out – redirecting when lost in thought streams» technique quite a few times before. So we will do it one more time, and we will go through the uncomfortable visit of this «guest» then out and back into focus. All we need is to trust the process and breathe.

None of these emotional intelligence «secrets» had been heard of when my teaching career began back in 1993. Never

I wish emotional intelligence had been a subject at my school

mind when I was a student myself! I wish emotional intelligence had been a subject at my school. We didn't use to have the tools that we have today to help all those brilliantly outstanding students who, very sadly, never showed up in the last minute, because of utmost stress (1) to give a speech (2) in public (3) in a foreign language (4) before three examiners in those days. The stories have been absolutely bizarre sometimes... from students (adults) on valium for the speaking test to sudden fainting in the rooms. I will never forget this police officer who put Me on guard actually when I noticed how the shakes, the sweat and the stress had taken over and sadly failed to complete the speaking task. Amazingly enough the same person that «gave me a fright» that afternoon when they first turned up in the classroom officially dressed in this rather intimidating uniform.

Focus

So let's keep moving and breathing. Let's welcome those signs of stress in our body and breathe, then slowly and gently consciously re-direct and focus on what brought me here today: to deliver a monologue in foreign language before these examiners. And as I have all my notes here in front of me I can manage to speak out the phrase that I have practiced, practiced, practised a million times before: «I am going to talk about» or «My monologue is about» or «I would like to begin by saying that». Once we are on the move the words will flow at their own pace. Perhaps a little unsteadily at first but most probably fluently once the wheels are in motion and the ideas noted on your paper are being put through. And remember that every time an episode of stress comes back to the examination set, I know I can follow the same procedure over and over again until I get through to the end of the task, which is in fact only three minutes.

*Acceptance of what we feel
helps reduce stress.
Awareness minimises impulsivity
increasing self-regulation*

Session five: exam time management

We can now focus on managing our time during exam hours to help us relax and focus improving our results in standardised English tests.

Being an insecure candidate at examinations when I was a student myself, I can strongly relate to all those students who do have a hard time when sitting exams. Here are some tips that I have ensembled to release those uncomfortable tensions that may prevent us from having the best outcome possible.

Speaking tests

I have always recommended students to record their monologues and dialogues regularly to gain practice for the final speaking tests, by acting as «their own examiners». Amongst the benefits are: (1) growing more aware of how much time you actually have to devote to the items you would like to present the examiners on the topic you have been given; and (2) finding out what can get improved after you have watched your video recording several times, namely (a) is the speech clear, (b) did you make yourself understood, (c) were the ideas introduced and developed in an organised manner, (d) was it a dull and empty monologue or interesting and exciting on the contrary, (e) was the language appropriate for the level certificate you would like to achieve or can you use more accurate grammar structures and expressions, (f) was the task interactive and well balanced in the case of dialogues, for instance. TEDx talks are fantastic resources to model public speeches.

Observation brings awareness

The criteria your examiners will be checking during your performance can be found in the official instructions published yearly by the Institution, and the suggestion is that ...you become your own examiner at times during the academic year or work with your classmate on a regular basis to exchange feedback.

So after you have practiced, practiced, practiced throughout the academic year, try to get to the examination room today as naturally calm as posible. Safe place practice audios available, which may help before you walk into the room, and simply try to forget about everything around you at this moment and focus on yourself (who have practiced a lot in advance) sitting there, getting your tasks prepared comfortably and confidently. Remember you will be allowed fifteen minutes to prepare both your speaking tasks and will need three to four minutes to deliver your monologue, then five minutes to discuss your dialogue topic with your partner (seven minutes if small group of three).

Improved attention is one of the benefits of our long standing attention regulation practices so our concentration skills in preparation for this test today are high. Also we are opening spaces for Emotions here so the recommendation is for you to embrace an emotion when it comes, seek help if you feel the need to ask for something to the examiner (maybe sitting by a window to breath some fresh air, or drink a little water) and Normalize it. Take your time to come back to the line of speech in case of an uncomfortable blank as we learned in our emotion regulation practices.

Written test

As you may have checked in the Official Instructions, the timings for your examinations are **strict** in an attempt to give all national candidates the same opportunities. I will not take much of your time on useful tips to complete your Reading Comprehension tasks except for a reminder of your **focus and concentration** skills acquired throughout *befriending silence* practices. Remember to read the questions first as this is not a reading for pleasure exercise, we are actually **scanning** this text looking **for answers** to follow up questions. Skimming all Reading Comprehension paper exams first to decide where to start could be a good technique (perhaps it works well for you to complete the most difficult exercise first).

Do not forget to breathe!

The same applies to your Listening Comprehension test: **skim** the questions first, underline seemingly key words, take notes during first listening, which might be connected to the answers, answer questions during second listening and finally complete the test before handing in. My long experience with students during Listening Comprehension tests is that they tend to tick the correct answer (A,B,C or D) the first time, however, too many times they change their minds before handing in. In high percentage this last minute change happens to be ruinously inappropriate so my advice is to go with your gut feeling as most of the times that first choice is correct. Mindfulness practitioners will be aware of this third brain connectivity in decision making.

Do not forget to breathe!

As for your written production test, (a) read the tasks carefully and take notes, (b) write a first draft to begin with (breaking your ideas into paragraphs, using the correct format and cohesive devices to keep your writing organised), (c) be mindful of time including in your planning to allow yourself a few minutes for a final fair copy to get written (the examiners will certainly appreciate **nicely presented** written tasks), (d) use your cognitive flexibility skills acquired through previous mindfulness practices to **be creative** when you write, (e) eventually, adjust the number of words wisely. You may like to have a look at the link with recommendations provided. I encourage you to go back to your «safe place» if you need so during short pauses, as leaving the room is not permitted unless exceptional circumstances are given. Our regular practice will have built up your patience as it is one of the multiple benefits of Mindfulness. You can ***create a silent space*** in which to find the natural regulation of emotions and Stay Calm. Be mindful. The result will **be f-e-n-o-m-e-n-a-l** recommendations.

Nice work!

Session six: cultivating resilience

Resilience and Loving Kindness come in one package the way I see it. When we believe we have tried our best (in this case «sitting an exam») and the result is not what we expected our self-esteem begins to suffer. Connecting resilience to self compassion practices makes sense as we will be addressing a key issue here: to take care of and send love to ourselves.

The definition of compassion is a *strong feeling of sympathy and sadness for the suffering or bad luck of others and a wish to help them.* We seem to forget though that we can show ourselves that same strong feeling of sympathy and wish to help. This is called self-compassion. Where our self esteem most of the time grows up with others showing their admiration and recognition, self-compassion practices can help us pull ourselves back together and make us more resilient. Imagine for example, you were to show empathy to someone else who has failed by imagining what it would be like to be in that person's situation, what would you (not) say to them? how can you build up your ability to share their feeling and experience? and in what way would you encourage them to keep trying? As it happens, what is (actually not) funny about this is that we are perfectly prepared to support others when they fail, however, this inner voice abashes us by criticising and diminishing our own achievements.

There is no doubt you can actually stop that inner voice that is beating yourself up by sending all those unnecessary messages and start relating to yourself kindly like Dr Kristin Neff explains in the videoclip available. Tell «your friend» that it was worth trying because they are now actually more aware of how much they know and how much they don't know, that they mustn't give up just because their speaking exam was «disastrous», you can say that practice makes perfect and they need to try again, you can invite them to go celebrate those parts they did pass, you can help «your friend» set up a plan for the next exam submission dates, or you can help them take perspective, after all it is just an exam!

> *The proposal is to practice self-love exercises to recover from failure and get back to learning. Instead of the usual self-criticism practice, we can start growing more resilient today by showing empathy and encouragement to ourselves as if to our best friend...*

How about «Writing yourself a compassionate letter» to increase your inner strength? Drop yourself a few lines to boost self compassion, imagine you are writing this letter to a dear friend, what kind words would you say to them? One other favourite practice is to Look at that person in the mirror (see #LovingKindness ahead) that you can adapt to this imaginary exercise of talking to «your friend» if they have failed their important examination.

You can also hug «your friend» and tell them they will still be your friend even if they never become bilingual ... we often seem to live with a sense of not being good enough and feel the need to compete, outperform others, achieve more, be perfect ... and we don't stop to consider whether our self-critical and competitive attitude is actually helping us achieve these goals or whether it might actually be standing in our way. Self-compassion actually leads to increase productivity once we have managed to decrease stress.

Session seven: loving kindness

Very closely related to the previous session is this Loving Kindness practice magnificently exemplified by Luc Besson (Angel A - 2008). In the videoclip available Die Rasmussen asks her friend James Debbouze to look at his reflection in the mirror and try and be loving and appreciative of himself.

Loving Kindness practices work with the quality or feeling of kindness directed at ourselves, directed at our own experience, at our own life. Within the context of Mindfulness practice, Kindness it's not just an idea, it is quite a bit deeper than simply the thought that we should be nice to people or nicer to ourselves. Kindness is actually something we feel, and we can use our thoughts and intentions to cultivate the feeling.

So Loving Kindness and Self-compassion practices are two sides of the same coin, and as explained before, the intention is to build up our own strengths that help with facing up adversity.

Session eight: closing up

We seem to have come to the final session where I would like to narrate what we have been trying to learn since we first met for session one. The intention of this «Be Mindful» proposal has been to give L2 students *skills* for developing their ability to focus and concentrate when they have this feelings of being out of focus, of anxiety and/or frustration before – during- after their *public speaking* examination. The acquisition of these preventive skills will be of interesting use and can be applied as well to a variety of scenarios in their academic life and also out of their academic life as the trainees admitted after the original implementation program.

The first step is to fully understand why we are doing all this, as it was described in the opening session «from doing to being». To build up our concentration skills we need to realise that to be able to sit *still and concentrate* we first need to be able to stop and sometimes we are not capable of doing that. We find it difficult and at times impossible to go from doing things 24/7 to simply «being», which is why we have been offered some *befriending silence* practices. Once accustomed and not uncomfortable with sitting still in silence for a few minutes «doing nothing» we will be fully prepared to grow more aware of what is happening around and inside of us through *focusing-on-breathing* techniques.

Mastering these focus-on-breathing practices will lead us to begin paying attention to and **managing** our feelings of stress or anxiety through *observation* of what is happening around and inside of us: *attention regulation* and *emotion regulation* techniques.

Be Mindful activities climax in *session five* when students reach the important meeting with the examiners (to deliver their monologues and dialogues) where they will now be able to overcome those «unwanted guests» that most unexpectedly block their progress.

A set of follow-up activities finally complement this Be Mindful proposal for L2 students learning how to manage stress during exam time, which focus on growing *more resilient* towards failure and exercising *less self-criticism* actions to increase productivity.

Emotional Intelligence practices have proven hugely effective with Primary to Baccalaureate pupils, and the fact that Mindfulness interventions and programs are also being carried out at *prestigious universities* gives us good evidence of the *positive impact* these learning strategies can have *on adult education* schools whatever the discipline, language, art, sport, etc.

Programs and Interventions of Mindfulness in Education

So that it can better be understood how Mindfulness practices can help schools all over the world I am pleased to share part of my final research work that completed my Master's studies in Emotion Regulation through the practice of Mindfulness, with worldwide programs and interventions applied in the Educational field:

1. MBWE Mindfulness Based Wellness Education is an 8-week program for teachers based on MBSR. The program teaches formal mindfulness practices as a foundation for cultivating an awareness of one's health or ill-health in the physical, social, mental or emotional domains of human existence. It is designed as a health promotion intervention for individuals who are at risk of developing stress related problems or the like, such as burnout. The interventions have proven effective in reducing psychological distress and augmenting satisfaction with life.

2. CARE Cultivating Awareness and Resilience in Education helps teachers handle their stress and rediscover the joys of teaching. The program offers teachers and administrators tools and resources for reducing stress, preventing burnout, enlivening teaching and helping students thrive socially, emotionally and academically. Participants learn how to

- recognise and regulate their own emotions and other's
- build up awareness
- be more present and engaged
- active-listen to others and
- become more compassionate in order to
- optimize opportunities of healthy emotional contact and understanding of others

3. SMART Stress Management and Relaxation Techniques in Education supports participants in re-connecting to personal/professional meaning and purpose, finding balance, cultivating emotional intelligence, and improving mental and physical health. Research results show that participants who complete the program experience:

- more focused attention
- increased working memory capacity
- reduced occupational stress and burnout
- reduced feelings of anxiety and depression
- greater mindfulness
- higher levels of self-compassion

The program focuses on teachers and is also complemented with MindUp [see www.mindfulenglish.net]. It involves experiential activities in mindfulness including: meditation, emotional awareness movement presentations and group discussions.

4. Mindfulness Matters well-known as The Eline Snel method (2013) addressed to Education and Health environments. Participants learn to stabilise, focus and shift their attention based on kind, attentive approaches. They become familiar with their inner- world, without having to make any immediate judgements about what they (or others) think, feel or experience. They learn to deal with calm and turmoil when these present themselves. And to acknowledge troublesome thoughts and feelings without burying them away or getting carried away by them, but simply giving them some kind of attention. Last but not least, they learn to be kind to themselves and others.

5. ABC Attention, Balance and Compassion: the Inner Kids Program trains participants on:

- Mindfulness of Body = bringing awareness, attention, or focus to breathing and bodily sensation.

- Mindfulness of Feeling = noticing the affect tone, such as pleasure or displeasure, that comes with every sense object, whether a sensation or a thought.
- Mindfulness of Mind = noticing when there is attachment (greed, judgement, wanting) present in the mind and when there is not attachment present.
- Mindfulness of Mental Objects/Phenomena = being mindful and attentive to any thought that arises and allowing it to pass away unobstructed, and eventually directing this observance through a much more in depth exploration of the true origins of that thought.

6. IRP Inner Resilience Programme focuses on integrating social and emotional learning (SEL) with contemplative (mindfulness) practice. Founded by Linda Lantieri in 2002 in response to the effects of the September 11 attacks on New York City, the program was designed

- to provide school staff and parents with the skills and support needed to rebuild their inner strength and resilience,
- and in doing so be better able to support the children in their care.

IRP includes professional development workshops on topics such as anger management, conflict resolution, self-care, and stress reduction. Results of research study show decreased stress and increased mindfulness in teachers, and decreased frustration and increased autonomy in students as a result of the IRP program.

7. Learning to breathe is a secular program which integrates certain themes of mindfulness-based stress reduction

(MBSR) developed by Jon Kabat-Zinn, into a program that is shorter, more accessible to students, and compatible with school curricula. It tailors the teaching of mindfulness to the developmental needs of students to help them understand their thoughts and feelings and manage distressing emotions. By learning important mindfulness skills students will learn to

- improve emotion regulation,
- reduce stress,
- improve overall performance, and
- most importantly, develop their attention.

8. MiSP Mindfulness in Schools Project is a national charity aiming at helping a generation of young people and children grow up with stronger foundations on mental health. By doing quality face-to-face teaching in the classroom teachers get trained in Mindfulness practices and given the opportunity to reconnect with why they began teaching in the first place step back from all those issues taking so much mental space and energy and reconnect with all those things that people go into teaching for and really enjoy like being creative in the classroom and with student.

The practices include variations of "The Three-minute breathing space", Bodyscan, Mindful eating, Mindful movements, Mindful texting, Thoughts and Sounds.

9. MS Mindful Schools works on research and resources to help school administrators, staff and parents understand the impact of Mindfulness practices. The following benefits of Mindfulness practice have been found by scholarly research:

- Improved attention: numerous studies show improved attention including better performance on objective tasks that require extensive concentration span.
- Emotional regulation: mindfulness is associated with emotion regulation across a number of studies, mindfulness creates changes in the brain that correspond to less reactivity, and better ability to engage in tasks even when emotions are activated.
- Greater compassion: people randomly assigned to mindfulness training are more likely to help someone in need and have greater self-compassion.
- Reduction of stress and anxiety: mindfulness reduces feelings of stress and improves anxiety and distress skills when placed in a stressful social situation.

10. MindUp by The Goldie Hawn Foundation, is a simple to implement and evidence-based program that is built upon four pillars to promote positive mental health and well-being:

1. Neuroscience: students learn about the concept of neuroplasticity and how their brain regulates emotions.
2. Positive psychology: the program infuses evidence-based strategies from the field of positive discipline to help students thrive and bolster their well-being.
3. Mindful awareness: students learn and practice mindful awareness to develop focused attention, emotional balance and well-being social.
4. Emotional learning: students are offered opportunities to practice developing SEL skills, referring to how individuals acquire the knowledge, attitudes, and behaviours needed to develop self-awareness, self-management, so-

cial awareness, relationship skills and responsible decision making.

11. Staf Hakeshev program uses Mindfulness practices to teach school staff, students and their families how to value the importance of pausing to improve cognitive learning skills, to develop emotional skills and pay attention to the inner world.

12. Still Quiet Place is a place of peace that is alive inside all of us and can be found by just closing our eyes and breathing. An eight-week mindfulness-based stress reduction program [MBSR]. It teaches stress management skills early in life that will help kids and adolescents grow into healthy adults by developing their natural capacities for emotional fluency, respectful communication, and compassionate action. It has helped countless participants achieve improvements in attention and resiliency, and reduce anxiety. By showing how to pay attention to life experience here and now with kindness and curiosity, and to experience the natural quietness that can be found within.

13. Wellness Works in Schools believes that mindfulness fortifies our natural human capacity for awareness and self-care. Being able to pay attention, self-regulate and learn leads to success, no matter our past experiences.

Mindfulness fosters health:

a. mental health: attention, learning, problem-solving, initiating and inhibiting, flexibility and following instructions;
b. emotional health: self-awareness, self-efficacy, self-calm-

ing, self- regulation, emotional intelligence, resilience;

c. somatic health: connecting behaviour to consequences, multisensory experiences, balance, body control and conscious, movement, interoception, stability; and

d. social health: social cognition, relating and connecting, detecting cues (verbal and non-verbal) understanding eye-contact, situational awareness.

Programs and interventions in Spain available in www. mindfulenglish.net

Acknowledgements

I have to say there are so many people and situations I feel obliged to acknowledge having contributed to this guide that it is difficult to be brief.

The first mention has to go to <u>Emotional Intelligence Speaking Activities for ESL Classrooms</u> (my first publication) which set me on the rails of collecting work that was being done anonymously and share it worldwide with other teachers who like me chose to innovate in a different direction.

When everyone else seemed to be experimenting with all sorts of digital technologies this "nutty professor" was more focused on experiencing thoughts, feelings and emotions management, and how best perform in a mindful genuine manner. In the era of "Insta Lies" I was asking my students to *genuinely* connect with *what* they needed to say and *how* they wanted to present that in the best possible manner. <u>Be Mindful</u> came next very naturally, as a toolkit of strategies our students could develop with a focus on excellency in their academic results. The motto being "decreased stress - increased productivity".

My students must be named too, of course, without them Be Mindful wouldn't have been possible. As well as my trainers and peer teachers from all over the world with whom I have shared hours of mindful moments.

Special appreciation to the University of Málaga for putting together the Postgraduate Masters Degree in <u>Emotion regulation through the practice of Mindfulness</u> where I discovered that it all finally fell into place.

Bibliography

Asunción (2018) Mindfulness en nuestro centro. Retrieved from https://youtu.be/ bG4afMALWlM

Avis, R.P. (2019) Empirically supported benefits of Mindfulness. Retrieved from https://www.apa.org/monitor/2012/07-08/ce- corner

Body, L. (2004) The Lotus That Blossoms on the Camino: A Spiritual and Therapeutic Journey to Santiago de Compostela through the Chakras. books.google.com›books

Body, L., Diaz, N. R., Recondo, O., & del Río, M. P. (2016). Desarrollo de la Inteligencia Emocional a través del programa mindfulness para regular emociones (PINEP) en el profesorado. Revista interuniversitaria de formación del profesorado, (87), 47-59.

BBC World news (2013) Mindfulness in Schools. Retrieved from https://youtu.be/ N8M5MJdXvJc

Brown, ET. (2005) The Unfocused Mind, NY Integrated Publishing.

Dhiravamsa, Dharmapadipa (2013) Un atajo a la iluminación: guía para la práctica de la atención plena, La Llave.

Doria, J.M., (2012) Meditación transpersonal: 101 claves de meditación y Mindfulness, books.google.es

Ekman, P (2012), Mindfulness: How to call off the emotional attack dogs, retrieved from "https://www.youtube.com/QG3fOOT7xWQ"

Frankl, V (2008), Man's search for meaning, books.google.com

Gascón, M. (2018) Creciendo con Mindfulness, books. google.com

GOV.UK (2019) Mindfulness en 370 centros británicos. Retrieved from https://www.gov.uk/ government/news/one-of-the-largest-mental-health-trials-launches-in-schools

Harper, A (2019) How teachers can help students reduce test anxiety. Retrieved from https://www.educationdive. com/news/how-teachers-can-help-students-reduce-test-anxiety/551507/

Jiménez, Ó (2019) Mindfulness: 6 beneficios inmediatos y Descubre algunos mitos sobre Mindfulness. Retrieved from https://oliverjjimenez.wordpress.com/

Kabat-Zinn, J (2016) Mindfulness para afrontar el estrés y la enfermedad. Retrieved from https://youtu.be/mmdqidh3-N4

Kabat-Zin, J. (2009) Wherever you go, there you are. Hachette Books

Menéndez, G (2018) La gestión del estrés a través del Mindfulness en el ámbito educativo. Retrieved from https://drive. google.com/open?id=12aPqqzQ71YMeZZ76jWCpuSgxI_ZKjbhm

Mindful Schools. Retrieved from https://www. mindfulschools.org/

Miller, CJ (2018) Testing a quick mindfulness intervention in the university classroom. Retrieved from https://www. tandfonline.com/doi/abs/10.1080/0309877X.2017.1409 345?journalCode=cjfh20&

MiSP (n.d.) Proyecto en Mindfulness para la Educación. Retrieved from https:// mindfulnessinschools.org/mindfulness-in- education/what-is-it/

Neff, K (2013), The space between self-esteem and self-compassion retrieved from TEDx "https://www.youtube.com/IvtZBUSplr4"

PsicoTools (n.d.) Las mejores universidades apuestan por el Mindfulness contra el estrés. Retrieved from https://psicologiaymente.com/meditacion/universidades-mindfulness-contra-estres

Publishing Butler, J (2018) When is a time Mindfulness helped you. Retrieved from https://youtu.be/KeVIqgDAP5Y

Ramos NS.; Enríquez, H. and Recondo, O. (2012), Inteligencia Emocional Plena. Mindfulness y la gestión emocional de las emociones. (Edición Revisada). Barcelona: Kairós.

Ramos Díaz NS. Proposal for a Compassionate Emotional Accompaniment Technique (CEAT) Based on Mindfulness to Manage Disturbing Emotions. OBM Integrative and Complementary Medicine, 2019;4(1):13; doi:10.21926/obm.icm.1901017

Ramos, N. (2019) The Mindfulness and Emotional Intelligence Program. Retrieved from http://www.lidsen.com/journals/icm/icm-04-01-017#1.2TheMindfulnessandEmotionalIntelligenceProgram(PINEP)

Santed, MA (2018) Mindfulness: fundamentos y aplicaciones Books.google.com

Sentis Brain Animation Series (2012) Neuroplasticity. Retrieved from https://youtu.bc/ELpfYCZa87g

Snel, E. (2013) Sitting Still like a Frog, books.google.com

Williams, M and Penman, D (2011) Mindfulness: a practical guide to finding peace in a frantic world, books.google.com

About the author

María Teresa Victoria Roura Vivas (1969) has been working as an English teacher for Official Language Schools in Junta de Andalucia, Spain, since 1993. For more than thirty years she has been implementing emotional intelligence activities in the classroom in an attempt to provide feelings of belonging and significance that build up her students' self-confidence in foreign language usage.

Her postgraduate Masters in Emotional Intelligence and Mindfulness at the Faculty of Psychology (University of Málaga, 2019) was a turning point on a personal and professional level. Amongst other creative works that followed up she gave shape to "Be Mindful: one easy guide on reducing anxiety and coping with examination stress".

* 9 7 8 8 4 1 8 9 1 2 5 8 0 *